CHOOSING THE RIGHT LAWYER IS NO ACCIDENT

A Guide to Personal Injury Claims

By Jeffrey Adelman, Esq.,

Florida Bar Board Certified Civil Trial Lawyer

(Revised 2025)

ISBN: 9781691209613

Disclaimer: Every case is different and unique. The information in this book is no substitute for consulting with a personal injury lawyer. No attorney-client relationship is established between you and my firm by your possession of this book or any of the information in it.

DEDICATION

I dedicate this book to wife Jessica and my sons Benjamin and Jacob. They give me the strength and courage to continue to fight for justice for my clients.

TABLE OF CONTENTS

PREAMBLE

If you are reading this, you likely have been injured as a result of a car accident or slipping or tripping on someone's premises as a result of negligence. In the pages that follow, I will provide insight as to what you should expect from a lawyer (attorney) fighting on your behalf for personal injuries. This book is intended as a general guide if you are unfortunate to have had this happen to you. It has been with the least amount of "legalese" as possible, so you do not have to be a lawyer to understand it.

Lawyers who represent the injured the right way know that it's extremely personal and not just business. I'm proud to be a personal injury lawyer fighting for people who have suffered serious injuries as a result of the careless conduct of others, and holding defendants accountable.

As a personal injury lawyer, I've heard just about every lawyer joke. My friends feel compelled to share each new one with me. I get it. We don't have the best reputation. The public is bombarded by over the top commercials on television, and you can't go far on the highway without seeing one injury billboard after the other. Unquestionably, personal injury attorney advertising has harmed the public's opinion of this area of the law.

But just like not all doctors, teachers or any other group are the same, the same goes for personal injury lawyers. Many of us genuinely care about our clients as individuals, and doing the best possible job for them. That calling goes far beyond just a payday.

If you are unfortunate enough to have been involved in an automobile accident or a slip/trip and fall incident, I wish you a speedy recovery and hope this guide will relieve some of your stress when entering this unfamiliar world.

Disclaimer: Every case is different and unique. The information in this book is no substitute for consulting with a personal injury attorney. No attorney-client relationship is established between you and my firm by your possession of this book or any of the information in it.

AUTOMOBILE INSURANCE BASICS

It is important to have a basic understanding of automobile insurance BEFORE you have an accident.

Automobile insurance varies from state to state. **Bodily Injury Liability** coverage, referred to as "BI," is the coverage you will most likely deal with if you bring a personal injury claim. In the event that you are at fault for an accident, BI protects you from having to personally pay for damages if the victim of your negligence has a personal injury claim. Believe it or not, Florida does NOT require drivers to purchase this coverage. It is the only state that does not require drivers be responsible and have coverage in the event that they hurt someone. In 2022, the Florida legislature overwhelmingly passed a bill that would have eliminated mandatory Personal Injury Protection (PIP) coverage and made bodily injury coverage mandatory. Unfortunately, Florida's governor vetoed the bill. I will discuss "PIP in more detail later in this chapter.

This is how it works. If you look at a policy and it says $50,000/$100,000, this means $50,000 per person, $100,000 total per accident. If there are more than two people injured, the total amount the insurance company can be on the hook for is still $100,000.

You are also not required by law in Florida to have any **Uninsured/Underinsured Motorist coverage,** referred to as "UM," in the event somebody hits you who does not have insurance or has a very small bodily injury insurance policy. But based on the information in the preceding paragraph, it is easy to understand why I strongly feel *this is the most important coverage on your policy.* Whatever amount of coverage you have on your own policy to help other people that you may have injured, your **bodily injury coverage** (BI), you can match that amount for your Uninsured Motorist Coverage.

You are only allowed to have UM coverage if you purchase BI coverage. For example, if you buy $50,000 in BI, then you are allowed to purchase up to $50,000 in UM coverage.

There is a way to increase your Uninsured Motorist Coverage above your bodily injury maximum limits. If you have more than one vehicle in your household, you can purchase something called **stacking**. Stacking coverage means that you can take the amount of vehicles in your household and multiply the amount of coverage you currently have by that number.

For example, by stacking, that same $50,000/$100,000 policy, multiplied by three vehicles, turns into a $150,000 per person, $300,000 per accident policy in UM benefits. Whatever amount of uninsured motorist coverage you have, you multiply that coverage by the number of vehicles in your household. If you are already purchasing uninsured motorist coverage, and you have multiple vehicles, this added protection could be extremely helpful if you have a serious crash.

If you don't have UM coverage right now, after you finish reading this section, **call your insurance company immediately and add it!** If you are driving on Florida roads, and you're seriously injured by somebody who isn't responsible enough to have coverage for their own negligence, you could be in some serious trouble. Medical bills are just the start. What if you can't go back to work if you were injured as well? Uninsured motorist coverage is critical even if it is not required insurance in your state.

Now let's discuss **Personal Injury Protection** coverage, referred to as "PIP." Every driver in Florida has to have PIP. It is required in Florida, but the vast majority of states do not require this coverage. I will explain how it works. Let's say you're in an accident, you're hit from behind and you're injured. **PIP coverage** will be your first available compensation. That's the first $10,000 of medical coverage to pay for any medical treatment needed as a result of injuries from the accident. It can also pay up to 60 percent of lost wages. Total PIP coverage is capped at $10,000 whether used for medical bills or lost wages.

Importantly, PIP benefits follows the person in most cases. For example, let's say Luke and Leia are traveling in a vehicle and the driver, Luke, causes an accident that injures both of them. If Leia owns a vehicle, her PIP benefits go through her own insurance company, and Luke's PIP benefits go through his policy. This is the case even though Leia was not driving. Now if Leia did not own a vehicle and nobody in her household owned a vehicle, then she could get benefits from Luke's policy.

You can also purchase **Medical Payments** coverage, often called "Med Pay" for short, which gives you supplemental coverage above the $10,000. You can get this additional coverage in amounts of $1,000 or more above the $10,000 PIP coverage cap. Just like any other coverage, the more coverage you want, the higher your premium will be.

If you have health insurance, Med Pay may not be necessary, because it will kick in in after the $10,000 of PIP benefits is used up.

Collision Coverage is another good option that you should have on your policy. Collision coverage means if the person that hits you does not have insurance or if they don't have adequate insurance, your insurance pays to get your car repaired or replaced.

Collision coverage has nothing to do with personal injury, only property damage. If you don't have this coverage on your policy and there's a dispute as to liability (who caused the accident), you'll have to wait until that liability dispute is resolved before your car is taken care of. Whereas if you have collision coverage, you can get the car repairs paid for by your insurance company right away, and your insurance company can go after the other insurance company later to recover the money that they paid out to repair your car, as well as any deductible you might have. This is called subrogation. Even if the accident is your fault, your insurance company is still responsible to repair your vehicle or pay for the value of the vehicle if the car is declared a total loss.

Comprehensive Coverage involves incidents that don't involve a car accident such as a tree falling on your vehicle, vandalism or hitting an animal.

Property Damage liability coverage, along with **PIP** coverage, are the only two requirements under Florida law. Property damage coverage compensates for someone else's property in an accident caused by your negligence, not your own. The terms "full coverage" or "complete coverage" that insurance agents throw around cavalierly are meaningless phrases, and I cannot help but cringe every time I hear a new client say they have it. It's sort of like saying "I'm wearing shoes." What kind of shoes are you wearing? Are they Nikes, Ecco, Kenneth Cole, or Crocs? High heels, sandals, cleats? If your agent says "this is for full coverage," ask questions!

Same with insurance. You have to know how much coverage you have, whether and when it could be helpful after an accident, and how much it will help you and your family in the event of a physical and/or financial catastrophe. If you have only $10,000 of UM coverage and you end up needing surgery, and lose 6 months of work, how far is $10,000 going to go in helping you?

Make sure your insurance agent is giving you good advice. Better yet, ask a personal injury lawyer that you trust to review your coverage with you. We are the experts.

YOU'RE IN AN ACCIDENT! WHAT SHOULD YOU DO?

It is estimated that between 5 to 6 million automobile collisions happen every year in the United States. It is important to have some basic knowledge of what to do if you are involved in a car accident, to make sure you protect your rights, health and finances. Here are 10 helpful tips if you are involved in a motor vehicle accident:

1. See if anyone in your vehicle is injured, as well as the other vehicle.

2. Call the police from the accident scene to report the crash. Do not rely on the other driver giving you insurance information, because the information he/she provides you may be wrong or incomplete.

3. Get the names, addresses and phone numbers of any and all witnesses. If someone stops at the scene to help you, thank them and ask for their information.

4. Take photographs of the vehicles and the accident scene if you are able to do so. If you have visible injuries, take photographs of them as well. If you have a "dash cam," make sure that footage is preserved.

5. Do not make any statements to the driver of the other vehicle concerning who is at fault for the accident.

6. If you are hurt, seek treatment with a hospital or medical provider immediately.

7. Call your insurance company to obtain a claim number, but DO NOT give a recorded statement if you have plans to hire an attorney.

8. Hire an attorney. It is in your best interests to hire a lawyer as soon as possible after an accident, as insurance companies try to take advantage of unrepresented victims of accidents. Insurance companies have been

known to ask accident victims to give recorded statements, or sign papers or liability releases that are potentially harmful to their claim before the full value of a claim is known. Injury claims are handled on a contingency basis, so you will not owe that attorney any money unless he/she makes a recovery for you.

9. Once you have hired an attorney, do not speak to ANYONE about any issue relating to your claim. If someone is questioning you, you should get their name, number, and who he/she represents and then direct them to speak with your attorney. And please, DO NOT post anything about your accident on social media!

10. Provide all documents, medical records, photographs or other potential evidence to your lawyer. Don't hold anything back. The defendant will find your prior medical treatment records. There are services such as ISO ClaimSearch that can alert defendants of your prior medical conditions and personal injury claims. Often, personal injury attorneys do these on their clients to make sure they are aware of their clients' past injuries to pre-emptively deal with prior issues. One of the biggest issues in personal injury claims are past accidents or injuries that a plaintiff did not disclose. Your credibility is everything. If the defense attorney thinks you are dishonest or lying, it will effect what they tell their client. This will influence how much money an insurance company or a business will offer you for your injury claim.

YOU'VE HAD A SLIP/TRIP AND FALL INCIDENT. WHAT SHOULD YOU DO?

Whether you have slipped and fallen in a supermarket or tripped over a hazardous defect in a parking lot, what you do next could affect the outcome of your personal injury claim for better or for worse. Here are 10 tips for what do after such an event:

1. If you are injured, seek medical attention as soon as possible.

2. If the fall happens at a business, it is important to notify the business of your fall immediately. If you don't tell them immediately and they don't hear about your incident for weeks or months, it impairs their investigation and can cast doubt on whether an incident actually occurred.

3. Take photographs and/or videos of what caused you to fall. Whether it is liquid on the floor or some type of object on the ground, preserve photographic evidence if you can.

4. Get the names and contact information of any witnesses to your incident. Additionally, get the names of any business employees that you interact with at the scene.

5. You are not required to write anything or sign anything at the premises where you fell. If you do write out a statement, get a copy of that statement. In fact, ask them if you will receive a copy before you write anything down or DO NOT agree to give it to them. It is normal for a store NOT to give you a full incident report as legally they don't have to, but anything you write or sign you are entitled to receive a copy of.

6. DO NOT SIGN ANYTHING RESEMBLING A RELEASE OF LIABILITY. Sometimes a business may try to have you sign a document where they will give you, say $500 in return for agreeing not to bring a personal injury claim against them. If you do this, you are forfeiting your right to make a claim for your full damages. **If in doubt, do not sign.**

7. Hire an attorney. Just like if you are involved in a car crash, it is in your best interests to get a lawyer involved as soon as possible, especially due to the complexity of premises liability cases like slip/trip and falls.

Investigators may need to go to the scene to obtain evidence before the negligent party cleans up or fixes the hazard. Time is of the essence!

8. Once you hire an attorney, do not speak to anyone from the other side without your attorney being present. If you receive phone calls, direct them to call your lawyer.

9. **Don't put anything about your incident on social media.** It can't help you, it can only hurt you.

10. Just like in automobile accident personal injury claims, you MUST provide all documents, medical records, photographs or other potential evidence to your attorney. The defendant will find your prior medical treatment records. Whether you are believable and being honest affects how much money a defendant will offer you for a personal injury settlement. Attorneys can guide you if they are aware of negative information. But if you fail to disclose this information even to your own attorneys, you could be risking your entire claim. Again, your credibility in a personal injury claim is everything.

ATTORNEY'S FEES IN PERSONAL INJURY CLAIMS

I want to take a moment to tell you about attorney's fees in personal injury cases. Personal injury attorneys are paid for their time and efforts on a contingency fee basis, which means that the attorney gets a percentage of whatever they collect. The standard fee in Florida is one-third of whatever's collected if the case is out of suit, which means no lawsuit was necessary because your claim was settled with the insurance company or the defendant amicably. If litigation is necessary, the contingency fee is 40%. If you get nothing, the attorney gets nothing. That's what working on a "contingency" means. It means that if an attorney is going to place your claim into lawsuit, they are going to be investing much of their time, money, and faith in you to prosecute your case.

When you are considering hiring an attorney, focus on questions like the following: Does the attorney actually litigate? Do they actually go to trial? Are they Board Certified in Civil Trial? Can I actually speak with the lawyer that I hire, or am I going to only be able to speak with assistants? The fees are standard in the industry. They are the same whether the attorney is an actual trial lawyer or not. If you are placing your trust in an advocate, it should be important to you whether they are capable of seeing the claim through to jury trial if necessary. It should be important to you whether you can actually talk to the lawyer. Just because a lawyer has more flashy advertisements than another lawyer is not any indication of what they are going to do for your case.

I'm proud to be among the less than 0.5% of all Florida Bar attorneys who can claim the distinction of being a battle-tested, Board Certified Civil Trial Specialist. Lawyers who are Board Certified have to take a test on their proficiency, and show that they have tried a sufficient amount of jury trials.

When clients put their faith and trust in a firm for their injury claims, they should know they are hiring attorneys who possess the ability to try their case if necessary. They should know that if the last offer from the defendant is unfair, that the attorneys they have hired are willing to go that extra mile of pleading their case in front of a jury.

Jeff Adelman, B.C.S., Esq.

WILL THIS ACCIDENT AFFECT MY INSURANCE RATES?

One of the most frequent questions I am asked by new personal injury clients is, "How will this accident affect my insurance rates?" The insurance companies have done a wonderful job of scaring customers away from using their insurance benefits, even though the insurance company cannot legally punish them for doing so, such as by raising rates. It is illegal for an insurance company to raise a customer's rates based on a "not at fault" accident. Do not buy into the urban legend that insurance companies have a right to raise your rates even when you are an innocent victim. An insurance company can be subject to paying attorney's fees and costs if it conducts business in this fashion.

Florida Statute 626.9541(o)3.a. specifically states: *"(o)Illegal dealings in premiums; excess or reduced charges for insurance.— 3.a.Imposing or requesting an additional premium for a policy of motor vehicle liability, personal injury protection, medical payment, or collision insurance or any combination thereof or refusing to renew the policy solely because the insured was involved in a motor vehicle accident unless the insurer's file contains information from which the insurer in good faith determines that the insured was substantially at fault in the accident."*

If an insurance company conducts business in this fashion, it can be subject to attorney's fees and costs pursuant to Florida Statute 624.155 upon the filing of a Civil Remedy Notice. This would be a first party action against the client's insurance company, and would allow the client's attorney to seek attorney's fees and costs.

The key number here is THREE. Insurance companies can raise your rates or drop you if you have three claims within three years. Insurance companies identify all sorts of "benefits" as claims. I have seen insurance company argue that using "roadside assistance" benefits as making a claim. It may sound crazy, but if you have AAA Roadside Assistance, or something similar through your car manufacturer or another company, I would recommend using that rather than your automobile insurance benefit in this regard if your car breaks down or you require a tow for another reason based on this knowledge.

Jeff Adelman, B.C.S., Esq.

CHOOSING A DOCTOR OR MEDICAL PROVIDER

There are several things you should look for when you are choosing a doctor to handle your health care as a result of injury from an accident. You want to look at the quality of the medical provider. You want to see what the provider's experience has been, what other people say about this provider online, the reputation in the community. You also want to consider what kind of credibility this doctor will have in court. Will they be believable? Will a jury like this person? You need to be confident that this doctor is somebody who is willing to cooperate with your attorney. By cooperate, I mean:

Will they give a deposition? Will they cause unnecessary delays in your case by not providing your attorney with medical records? Will they charge your attorney (which really is charging you) an excessive deposition fee? Are their bills grossly inflated? All of these things matter.

It's great to have somebody who is an excellent physician or chiropractor, but if the person is going to make it harder to present your claim to the insurance company or a jury, that's going to affect your attorney's ability to get you a decent settlement or verdict on your case. Some doctors are purposely difficult to work with because they don't want to give depositions or have any involvement with personal injury claims.

You need to consider whether the person you are treating with not only cares about your health, but also about the impact this accident has had on your life. There are plenty of doctors in the community that are skillful practitioners and willing to testify on your behalf.

You didn't ask to be involved in an accident, but if you are involved, you have to consider how what you do affects your claim. You must consider who is going to be telling your story to support your claim. Lawyers can recommend doctors for you, and there's nothing unethical or illegal about that. However, you should also do your own research on the medical provider recommended by your lawyer. It is important to know whether your doctor are looking out for you not just medically, but legally too. Being injured affects so many aspects of a person's activities of daily living, beyond just treatment and your ability to work. It is important to make sure you are with practitioners that recognize the impact the personal injury event has had on your mental well being and your capacity for the enjoyment of life as well.

Jeff Adelman, B.C.S., Esq.

STATUTES OF LIMITATION

Statutes of limitation vary from state to state, but in Florida, Illinois and at least half of the country, if you don't file your personal injury lawsuit generally within TWO years of the date of the occurrence, you are time-barred from ever bringing an action for that accident and your injuries.

If you would like to see what the statute of limitations is for your injury claim, there is a helpful chart available on www.NOLO.com if you search "Civil Statutes of Limitation." Be sure to ask your attorney about how the relevant Statute of Limitation affects your Florida personal injury claim. If you are going to make a claim, don't wait out the calendar—file. Delay can hurt you and hurt your attorney's ability to give you immediate guidance.

"HOW LONG IS THIS GOING TO TAKE?" & "HOW MUCH IS MY CASE WORTH?"

When I first meet with a client, the usual questions I get are "How much is my case worth?" and "How long will it take to settle my case?" And the answer to both questions is always, "I don't know."

A truthful answer will depend on several different factors, the first being, how much insurance is available on the case compared to the injuries? Next, does the person have Uninsured/Underinsured Motorist coverage, in the event that they were hit by somebody who does not have coverage or limited coverage? If there's no insurance, then unfortunately, in Florida, generally lawyers cannot help the victim because attempting to retrieve money on a claim when somebody doesn't have insurance is like pounding sand. It's futile. There are more protections available to people in debt in Florida than any other state. Florida's "Homestead" law outlined in Article X, Section 4 of the Florida Constitution is a major reason why.

Assuming there's some sort of insurance available, these questions and more are what determine the value of a victim's claim: How serious are the injuries? Is the client finished with their treatment? Has the plaintiff required any injections or surgeries? Will they be in physical therapy for months or years? Will they be able to return to work soon, or ever? What kind of impact will these injuries have on the victim's activities in daily life?

What I generally tell clients when I first meet them is that it takes a good 4-8 months to figure out whether a case can be resolved without having to file a lawsuit, or if they need to take that next step of filing the lawsuit. Of course, there are exceptions to this: the biggest exception would be if somebody is going through surgery and we need to know how long until they can recover from that surgery. You wouldn't want to settle a case until all of the facts are known and a doctor can give an informed final opinion as to what effect these injuries will have on the rest of your life.

Jeff Adelman, B.C.S., Esq.

While it would be nice to know the answers to those questions in the beginning, it would be like opening a book and wanting to guess the ending. The chapters have yet to be written.

DANGEROUS INSTRUMENTALITY DOCTRINE

Under Florida common law, if someone lends their car to another driver, and the driver causes an accident, the owner is additionally on the hook just as if they were driving the vehicle themselves. This is due to the Florida doctrine known as **"Dangerous Instrumentality."** Keep that in mind the next time you lend your car to somebody, or if you are selling your car, make sure that it is titled to the new person immediately or you could potentially bear responsibility for somebody else's negligence.

Dangerous instrumentality means that if you are involved in an accident, and you are injured, you should look not only at the driver, but find out who the registered owner of the car is. As long as permission was given to the driver (the car was not stolen), the owner's automobile insurance will apply to any in-jury damages you suffer. For more information about Dangerous Instrumentality, see Florida Statute Section 324.021.

COMPARATIVE NEGLIGENCE

In March 2023, the law of Comparative Negligence changed significantly due to the comprehensive tort reform bill known as Florida House Bill 837. Florida used to be a pure Comparative Negligence state. What this means is that a jury determines percentages of fault for a particular accident. If it was a three-car accident, and vehicles 1 and 2 were at fault, a jury decides how much each vehicle is responsible for the harm to vehicle 3. In a two-car accident, the plaintiff themselves can be found responsible for a percentage of fault.

Prior to the law changing, whatever percentage of fault the plaintiff had for their accident was deducted from their verdict. Now, if the plaintiff is found to be more than 50% responsible for a car crash or for a slip or trip and fall accident, they get ZERO.

For example: Cody and John are involved in an accident at an intersection. Both of them claim that the other ran a red light. Cody is bringing a claim for personal injuries against John. A jury can determine that John is 98% at fault, 50% at fault, 45% at fault or any other percentage. Determination of liability does not have to be absolute. However, if John is 45% and fault and Cody is 55% at fault, John wins and Cody gets nothing.

So, if a jury awards $100,000 in damages to Cody, and Cody is found to be 2% at fault, his net jury verdict award is $98,000. If he were 50% at fault, the net verdict would be $50,000. But if Cody were to be found 55% at fault, he loses.

Comparative negligence is the law of the land in Florida, and in very serious injury claims, even if the plaintiff owns some of the fault for the accident, the damages can still greatly exceed the policy limits of the other party, and the insurance company must then pay the full amount of their policy limits.

However, it is extremely important in evaluating whether a claim will be successful to consider whether a jury may find the plaintiff over 50% at fault because even if it's 50.1%, the plaintiff loses the case.

DEMAND LETTERS

Usually prior to filing a lawsuit, an attorney will send a demand letter to the insurance company to try and get the case resolved. There are really two types of demand letters:

1. Where policy limits are inadequate (not enough insurance to pay for your losses)

2. When a client/patient has reached Maximum Medical Improvement, meaning the client is as healthy and as close to the way they were before the accident as they are going to be.

Inadequate Limits Policy Demands: This involves a serious injury with not enough insurance coverage. As soon as it becomes obvious, such as if the injury is a fractured wrist and there's only a $10,000 policy of liability coverage, I send a letter out and there's several reasons for doing that. The first one is if that's all the money there is available through insurance, you might as well go and get it. You don't want it sitting in the insurance company's bank account.

Prior to accepting these policy limits, we usually do an asset search to make sure that the person who caused the injury doesn't have anything that would be attachable (collectable). We also try to get an affidavit from the owner and driver of the vehicle that there are no additional insurance policies that potentially could cover this loss, or anything that we could force a sale of, in the event of a judgment. But most of the time when you're dealing with somebody who has a $10,000 insurance policy for liability, they're not going to have attachable assets.

So that's something that you have to consider. And when people say to me, "Well, can you go after the person for more than the policy limits?", I tell them there's a reason that OJ Simpson moved to Florida and it isn't because of the weather. To try and get assets from somebody in Florida is very, very difficult. I previously discussed the "Homestead" rule which basically says you can't force somebody to sell their home because they owe a money judgment. Florida is one of the best states for protecting your assets and debtors who owe others money certainly know that. It is a big incentive for them to be in Florida.

When you send out an inadequate policy limit letter, you're also looking at "bad faith." **Bad faith** involves an insurance company not acting in the best interests of their insured, when a reasonable insurance company would do so. Florida Statute Section 624.155 (1)(b)(1) specifically reads:

"Not attempting in good faith to settle claims when, under all the circumstances, it could and should have done so, had it acted fairly and honestly toward its insured and with due regard for her or his interests;"

For example, if Luke is going to be out of work for six months and his lost wages are going to greatly surpass $10,000 on the subject policy, it's very obvious that the insurance company should offer the money on behalf of their insured, Leia, to him. If they don't offer the money to Luke, then bad faith comes into play and there's the possibility of actually getting more money that exceeds the policy limits Leia has with her insurance company. I urge you to read the statute above again. That is the standard. What is in the best interests of their customer? What is in the best interests of the victim? It is not "What is in the best interests of the insurance company?"

If the insurance company doesn't conduct themselves based on what a reasonable person would do, then they could be on the hook for the entire judgment a jury were to give a plaintiff. It's very important to give the insurance company an opportunity to do the right thing, but if they don't, within a certain grace period depending on the situation, then there is potential for a "bad faith" insurance claim. Not "tendering" the limits to the accident victim in a timely manner is the proof of "bad faith."

Standard Demand Letters. The normal demand situation would be when a client finishes care and treatment from an accident. If there are adequate policy limits, your attorney sends a demand letter that summarizes the care and treatment of the injury victim, and the lawyer gives the insurance company an opportunity to make a reasonable settlement. If the client can get the case resolved without having to file a lawsuit, that's good for them, good for the attorney, and good for the insurance company.

Unfortunately, as we know, such a resolution often does not happen. If the demand letter doesn't move negotiations further and they attorney can't get the case resolved, the next step is to draft a complaint and file a lawsuit.

THE COMPLAINT: FILING A LAWSUIT

Nobody should want to be involved in a lawsuit, but sometimes it's unavoidable. However, just because a lawsuit is filed does not mean you are automatically going to trial. The vast majority of claims still settle, even if they are in lawsuit.

Filing a lawsuit can move the process closer to conclusion, but whoever you hire as your personal injury attorney has to have the skills to navigate the waters of litigation in the event that your claim must go all the way to a jury.

Once a Complaint (the lawsuit) is filed with the court, a Summons is issued in the name of the Defendant. Your attorney will then hire a Process Server to physically hand the complaint (serve process) to the Defendant individual or registered agent of the corporation. It does not have to actually be the Defendant. It can be their spouse, or anyone in the house who is at least 15 years old. It sounds archaic in the 21st century, but it is still the way things are done.

There may be situations where a person is hiding their whereabouts, or cannot be found, and there are ways of dealing with that as well such as service of the Secretary of State. I'm not going to go into detail about those situations in a layperson's guide to personal injury law, but if you really want to know, reach out to me.

Once the Defendant is served with the complaint, they have 20 days to file a response, referred to as an "Answer and Affirmative Defenses." "Affirmative Defenses" provide reasons why a defendant thinks they should not have to pay, or should not have to pay as much. The Complaint, Answer and Affirmative Defenses are called "Pleadings." Once the Defendant has responded, the next step toward is "Discovery."

Side note: When your case is filed, you may have heard repeatedly from your attorney that they were dealing with State Farm, Allstate, GEICO, or another automobile insurance company. But when you look at the complaint, the insurance company name is nowhere to be found. Here's why: When you bring a lawsuit for injuries, the insurance company is not the party that caused the accident. They are stepping into the shoes of their customer, the defendant. The law wants the jury to make their decision not based on ability to pay, but on the law. The school of thought is that a jury might award more money to an injured plaintiff if they knew there was an insurance company that would cover the money damages. Unfortunately, this sometimes has an opposite effect where jurors are concerned that the defendant may have to pay the money judgment personally, and it can influence verdicts. With that being said, if you see a lawsuit against a person for personal injuries, it is safe to assume that there is automobile insurance covering the defendant. If there were not, most Florida attorneys would advise not bring the lawsuit because as mentioned earlier, it is extremely difficult, often next to impossible, to collect from people individually in this state.

One of the only ways you would see an insurance company named in a personal injury case is if it is an Uninsured/Underinsured Motorist claim, where the negligent defendant had no or very little bodily injury liability coverage, as discussed earlier.

DISCOVERY (WRITTEN)

Discovery is the fact finding and investigation portion of your lawsuit. Both sides learn what facts will and will not be heard by a jury.

Just because something is discoverable does not mean it is admissible (meaning that a jury will see it) at trial. Even though things can be learned in the discovery process that will not be heard by a jury, they may lead to evidence that will be heard. However, discovery requests must have some relevance. The attorney making the request must reasonably believe that it will lead to potentially admissible evidence.

Written discovery includes interrogatories, requests for production and requests for admissions.

Interrogatories are questions answered under oath. They're questions that you receive from the attorney representing the opposite party on your case. You will prepare your answers with your attorney and will have to sign them in the presence of a notary. It is important to tell the truth to the best of your ability when answering these as leaving out information can potentially lead to you being impeached, meaning that you are an unreliable historian or being dishonest.

Common questions asked in interrogatories are your full name, if you've been known by any other names in your life, your birthday, your work history, your criminal history, where you've lived the past 10 years, any injuries that you've had in the past 10 years, any doctors you've seen in the past 10 years or even in your entire life. They are the basis for the deposition that you will have to give as a Plaintiff in a personal injury case, at a later time. We will discuss depositions in the "Oral Discovery" section following this one.

Requests For Production are written requests for documents in your possession that are necessary for the proof of the claim, or the defense of the claim by the opposing party. They could include photographs/videos of or around the time of the incident, medical records from the incident or medical records of past health conditions, in which case you'll be asked to sign a medical authorization as part of the investigation of the claim.

Requests For Admissions present the scariest written discovery to me, because they are statements written by the opposing attorney that must be admitted or denied within 30 days. If not, the statements are deemed admitted by law, and can be read to a jury at trial. You will have to admit or deny the truth of each of the statements that are presented.

If, by chance, your attorney misses the deadline, you can still get your admissions in late by a motion in front of the judge, but it's certainly quite embarrassing for any attorney that has had to do this. You want to get it right the first time.

Side note on tax returns: Do I have to disclose them? When you have a wage loss claim, your tax returns are discoverable by the other side. This can be a problem if you are somebody who relies on cash for income but has not reported all of it to the government on your income tax return. If a plaintiff makes a wage loss claim that includes unreported income when taxes have not been reported properly, the plaintiff would either have to lie about their tax returns or admit criminal conduct.

Therefore, if someone works with cash or does not report all of their income, they should not bring ANY type of wage claim. Waiving that claim makes the returns irrelevant, so you will not subject yourself to impeachment, perjury or criminal indictment.

Side note on Social Media: If your case is in litigation, resist the temptation to post! Facebook, Instagram, X, TikTok and other social media are discoverable meaning the defense will have access to look at it and question a plaintiff about it. Defense attorneys have the right to view this information, and they will! What you put something out there for public consumption assume you should be aware that you can be questioned about it at deposition and at trial.

Choosing the Right Lawyer is No Accident

Florida Bar Ethics Opinion 14-1 specifically offers some guidance for personal injury clients and their attorneys concerning social media:

"A personal injury lawyer may advise a client pre-litigation to change privacy settings on the client's social media pages so that they are not publicly accessible. Provided that there is no violation of the rules or substantive law pertaining to the preservation and/or spoliation of evidence, the lawyer also may advise that a client remove information relevant to the foreseeable proceeding from social media pages as long as the social media information or data is preserved."

With social media being a part of life for so many of us, plaintiffs and Defendants for that matter must be careful what they post. I have seen judges actually grant motions demanding that the injured party "friend" the defense attorney so they can look at a plaintiff's social media posts. Defendants are allowed to download all the photographs and posts on those pages.

I mentioned it before, but it bears repeating: **DO NOT write anything about your accident claim on social media.** One of my law professors put it this way, "Don't ever put something in writing you wouldn't want to see on the front page of the newspaper." I know referring to newspapers is a dated reference for many these days, but the idea of not putting things in writing on the internet or in print remains more true than ever.

VIRTUAL PROCEEDINGS (ZOOM, TEAMS, ETC.)

Since the COVID pandemic of 2020, most legal proceedings are conducted on Zoom or similar platforms. This includes hearings, depositions, mediations, non-binding arbitrations and more. You can always ask your attorney if you can come to their office and they can accommodate you. However, the other attorney and participants will likely still be on a screen. If you choose not to come to your attorneys office, here are some tips to make sure these proceedings move forward without technical problems and you can help yourself and your attorney by doing the following:

1. If possible, do not use your smartphone. You may have to view documents on your screen or photographs, and it is going to be difficult for you to see them on a small screen. A tablet or a computer is simply better.

2. If you are hooked up to a wired ethernet connection, that is preferable. However, at the very least you are connected to a strong Wi-Fi signal.

3. You must be somewhere private, and give your undivided attention to the proceeding. A room in your home or at work is fine. Some people have no choice but to do it parked in their vehicle (never while you are driving). Nobody is supposed to be with you while these events are happening. You should not be doing another activity such as doing the dishes (yes, I had a client do this during a mediation). Show respect for the process. Remember, the defendants and their attorneys are evaluating you as a witness and whether you will be likeable in front of a jury. Show that you are taking your claim seriously.

4. Make sure you have decent lighting. Do not have an open window behind you as it will distort your image. Lighting coming from behind your camera is better than light behind you when you are on video.

5. Test your equipment! Make sure you have a camera and microphone that work properly. If you haven't already, download Zoom or whatever platform you will be using in advance to avoid problems the day of your event.

Legal proceedings can be stressful on their own. Don't add to the stress by dealing with avoidable technical issues. This will allow you to focus on your claim so you can be at your best when you are going through a deposition or other matter.

DEPOSITIONS (ORAL DISCOVERY)

Now we are going to discuss depositions. You will be required to testify under oath and you can be asked about anything that passes the "could reasonably lead to discoverable evidence" test. It is normal to be nervous, but if you read this section and meet with your attorney, it should quell some of your anxiety before this very important moment in your claim.

It is critical that you tell the truth, and your personal injury attorney should meet with you and prepare you for as long as it takes until you are comfortable discussing your injuries and the event that caused your injury. It's ok to say "I don't know" if you're not sure of something. If you remember something later in the deposition, you should tell the questioning attorney that you want to go back to something you said and tell them that information.

If you need to take a break at any time during a deposition to go to the bathroom, take a smoke break, or go grab some water, all you have to do is ask. This is not a marathon. Your attorney will be with you as long as it takes to get this deposition done. Don't think that they are watching the clock. Remember, personal injury attorneys are working on a contingency fee. They only get paid if they settle your case or get a verdict for you.

Get a good night's sleep the night before your deposition. Take the day off so your boss does not have the expectation that you are going to be coming in to work. You must be able to answer the opposing attorney's questions as accurately as possible. You do not want to get **impeached** at trial, which means showing that you've said two different things at two different times under oath. In layperson terms, trying to paint you as a liar.

What follows are my rules for clients for the deposition preparation and how they should conduct themselves during this important proceeding.

JEFF'S DEPOSITION RULES

1. *If they don't ask, they don't get.* Get in, get out. No small talk. Answer the question and that's it. Nothing extra. You are not there to do the job for the defense attorney. You're there to answer their questions and leave. If they ask good questions, they will receive the information. This is their only opportunity to speak with you. You just answer what is asked. If they don't ask certain questions that you think are important, you don't want to volunteer that information. If you do leave something important out, your attorney has the chance to ask you questions after the defense attorney is finished, to clear up any issues. Don't talk too much!

2. *Larry's $100 Rule.* I had the privilege of practicing law with my father (Larry) for many years. He used to tell clients, "Every extra word you say costs you $100." That means you need to be short, sweet, and to the point with your answers. Remember, you don't need to fill the pauses with words. Just answer the question. In terms of the answers, if you don't know, there's nothing wrong with saying, "I don't know" or "I don't recall." Most of your answers should be "yes" or "no." Do not think out loud!

3. *Don't guess!* If you're not sure, say "I don't know," and if you don't understand the question, say "I don't understand." You could ask the defendant's attorney, "Can you please rephrase that?" or "Do you have something that could refresh my memory?" You can use words like "about" or "approximately" if you are not exactly sure such as for distance, time and/or speed. Importantly, you're allowed to have your sworn answers to interrogatories in front of you during the deposition, and you should. There's nothing wrong with saying, "I would defer to the medical records," if you can't remember a date or don't remember exactly what the doctor said. Let the records speak for themselves. Your doctor is going to explain your conditions better than you can anyway.

4. *Never say never or always.* You get no points for being emphatic when "yes" and "no" are perfectly acceptable. And what happens if the defense

has surveillance of you doing something you say you "never" do? Stay away from unnecessary, absolute words.

5. ***Counting Mississippis.*** I alternatively call this the "Thoughtful Pause Rule." For those of you that have played touch football, you know you can't rush the quarterback until you have counted Mississippi 3-7 times, depending on who makes the rules. It is essential that you take a thoughtful pause or count "Mississippis" to collect your thoughts before you speak and before any words come out of your mouth. This gives you a chance to think and additionally gives your attorney time to object if necessary. DO NOT cut off the defense attorney while they are questioning you. You may take the question in a different direction than the defense attorney intended and disclose something that the defense attorney would never have known but for you not following this rule. Let the attorney finish the question, count your "Mississippis," and only then answer. You should handle every single question this way. There is no rush. Take your time and give yourself a thoughtful pause before answering questions.

6. ***"OBJECTION!" means keep quiet.*** Your attorney is either making a legal objection and alerting you to pay close attention before answering. If you are following the "Mississippi rule," you shouldn't have a problem with this. However, you still may have to answer these questions. But the next rule talks about when you should not answer a question that is objected to by your attorney.

7. ***Attorney-client privilege.*** What you and your attorney talk about is off limits to the opposing attorney! This can include if your attorney referred you to any medical provider. Do not divulge ANYTHING your lawyer tells you. If your attorney uses this objection and tells you not to answer, you should not. This is another reason you must take a thoughtful pause before answering questions. You want to make sure the other attorney is not asking a question that they are not entitled to an answer to.

8. ***Review documents.*** You should review your answers to interrogatories AND these rules at least twice prior to your deposition. As I mentioned earlier, you may bring your answers to interrogatories with you to your deposition if you need to refresh your memory. Also, if you are taking a lot of prescription medications, or are worried that you

are going to forget to mention something, you can bring notes. But keep this to a minimum, because the defense attorney will be permitted to view anything you bring into the deposition.

9. *Keep your cool!* Do not get mad. As much as the information you are giving the defense attorney is important, your body language, your demeanor, everything about you is being evaluated from the perspective of "Will he/she be a good witness in front of a jury?" If the defense attorney is outrageous or inappropriate, that's what your attorney is there for. Some personal questions will be asked, and your reactions to them will be watched. Some common questions asked are: What is your marital status? Have you ever been convicted of a crime? What is your highest level of education? What do you do for work? What is your immigration status? Your attorney should make you aware of this ahead of time and you should disclose to your attorney any worries you have concerning facts or events from your life that you either concerned about discussing, or don't know how to talk about. Remember, attorney-client privilege exists so you can have an open and honest discussion with your attorney about anything and receive proper guidance. The time to bring them up any concerns is before the deposition. *Attorneys can help clients with just about any problem as long as they are made aware of it.*

10. *Tell the truth!* Don't "oversell." Depositions can be quite dry actually, and it's not your job to get the attorney to "see it your way" or entertain the defendant's lawyer. We all use exaggeration in everyday conversation, but depositions are under oath and those can be taken as untruthful or lying. Always tell the plain truth. There are two questions that are almost always asked by defense attorneys: a) Is there anything you cannot do anymore that you did before the accident? And b) Is there anything that you are more limited or restricted in doing since the accident? These are two very different questions. When they ask you if there is anything you can't do anymore, it means exactly that. Anything you CAN'T do anymore. If your life depended on it, you could not do it. Most plaintiffs are not going to have a lengthy list of things they can't

do anymore unless they have a very catastrophic type of injury. The limitations question requires a more lengthy answer. This could be continuing to do activities but taking more frequent breaks. Not doing certain activities because they hurt, but you could do them if you needed to. It is important to understand the distinction between these two questions.

Any person about to be deposed as a Plaintiff in a personal injury claim would be well served by following these rules, but they are no substitute for an in-person or virtual meeting with your attorney to prepare for the specific facts of a client's particular claim.

DEFENSE DOCTORS

Defense Doctor Expert Witnesses are often casually referred to as IMEs. I never let them be referred to as IMEs because IME stands for Independent Medical Examination. These doctors are paid expert witnesses for the defense and from the insurance companies and corporations, so to call them an independent medical examiner is simply untrue. The Courts say they are Compulsory Medical Examinations (CME) or Defense Medical Examinations (DME), and the term IME should never be allowed in your case.

Let's focus on the actual medical examination that will be performed on you, the accident victim bringing the lawsuit. This will be performed by the doctor who is being paid to come to court and testify AGAINST YOU at trial. They may likely testify that you were not hurt in the accident, that you are not as hurt as you say you are, that you are exaggerating, that you are lying, or possibly that if you have a painful condition or injury, it has nothing to do with the accident. They will say that your injuries pre-exist the accident. That the findings on the MRI are degenerative, meaning that they are the result of you getting older. The paid defense expert doctor may levy several of these opinions against you.

It is rare for these doctors to say that a Plaintiff is hurt in the subject car crash or slip and fall, so keep that in mind when you are going to the doctor visit. This is not like any doctor visit you have been to because this doctor is not there to help you and will tell you this. Next are my rules for conducting yourself at one of these defense doctor examinations.

JEFF'S RULES
ON DEFENSE DOCTOR PREPARATION

We recommend you follow these rules if a compulsory medical examination/ defense medical examination is scheduled.

Talk with your lawyer a few days before the exam. Prior to the CME, your attorney should speak with you to prepare you for this significant event in your case. They may go over the medical records with you, your written discovery responses, and go over what you can expect during the visit with the doctor.

All eyes are on you the moment you enter the doctor's office! From the moment you walk into the doctor's office, assume that you are being watched. For that reason, you do not want to get there an hour before. Fifteen minutes is just fine. In fact, if you are early, stay in your car until about 15 minutes before.

Say NO to doctor paperwork! If the defense attorney has not given your attorney any paperwork to fill out prior to the examination, don't fill out any paperwork at the doctor's office. NOTHING. This is not a standard medical examination. If your attorney has not seen the documents, you should refuse to fill them out. If the office insists, call your lawyer.

Be polite and cooperative, but not intimidated. You will want to be polite and cooperative of course, but understand that this doctor's examination will be different than any you probably have had before. You need to be confident and prepared in the defense doctor's office, and not intimidated by the doctor's white coat or the degrees on the walls. It's important to be respectful and tell the truth, but you need to understand the purpose of the examination. **The doctor is not there to treat you or offer any advice to you about your medical conditions.**

Dates aren't critical, but prior injuries are. The doctor should have all of your medical records. If you don't remember the date you saw this provider or that one, it is not a big deal. However, you should be prepared to talk about any prior car accidents or incidents, especially if they involve similar areas of the body. Honesty is a must. Also, those "Answers to Interrogatories" we discussed earlier? Bring those with you to help, along with a list of medications or doctors if you have difficulty remembering.

Video the examination. We try to send a videographer to every CME. Most Courts in Florida allow it. The doctor and his staff cannot prevent the client or attorney from filming the examination and cannot charge an additional amount of money to the client or their attorney for doing so.

It's also considered the Plaintiff's Attorney's Work-Product. That means that the defense cannot get a copy of it, except if your lawyer plans on showing it at trial.

The video is important because it shows, objectively, what happened during the examination. Sometimes these paid defense doctors will lightly or barely touch a client, and then write in their report something to the effect of "patient did not respond to palpation (touching)." This may be an attempt to deny that you are experiencing pain or discomfort from the accident.

Video makes sure that there is an accurate record of everything that happens, and everything that was said during these examinations. Injury lawyers don't trust these doctors just because they have a medical degree, and you should not either. Their purpose is to minimize and/or destroy your claim.

These "hired gun" doctors are part of an industry that allows them to make millions of dollars a year discrediting injured Plaintiffs, finding ways to give defendants an out not to pay what they should pay on claims. It's great work for them because they don't have to make any tough decisions and they have virtually no risk of medical malpractice if they are wrong.

All of these reasons together should demonstrate why a video of the defense expert witness doctor's examination of you is important. At no time should you allow the doctor to instruct the videographer to turn off the camera!

Problems? Call your lawyer! Have your lawyer's phone number with you in the event you need to call. If a client feels uncomfortable at the examination because of something the defense doctor says or is doing, I instruct them to call me, and I have listened to the remainder of the examination on speakerphone in these instances. If a client insists on their lawyer being at the examination, the lawyer should attend live, but having the video in most cases is enough to keep the defense doctor in line. Most of them have done these examinations hundreds or thousands of times before, are pretty smooth, and do not want a confrontation with the client or attorney at this stage of the litigation.

Contact your lawyer after the exam. Let the lawyer know how long you had to wait to be seen by the doctor. Did anyone else try to question you besides the doctor? The doctor and only the doctor you are scheduled to see should be asking questions. How much time did the doctor spend with you? How long did they spend with you asking questions? How long did the physical examination take? Did anything strange or unusual happen? Did the doctor say anything about your injuries that was potentially useful? (Doubtful.) In the event that the case does go to trial, some of this information could prove valuable, and best to jot it down while it's fresh in your mind.

PROPOSALS FOR SETTLEMENT

Proposals for settlement are valuable litigation tools to put pressure on parties to settle lawsuits. This strategy concerns Florida Rule of Civil Procedure 1.442, and involves assessing attorneys' fees and costs for a prevailing (winning) party or party that offered to settle a case prior to trial for a reasonable amount. At mediation, proposals for settlement almost always come up because one or both sides likely has sent one or more of these to their opponent.

The rule states that if the defendant in a litigation files a "proposal for settlement" under Florida Rule of Civil Procedure 1.442, **the plaintiff must obtain a verdict of at least 75 percent of the amount proposed by the defendant.** If there is a defense verdict or the verdict is less than 75 percent of the verdict, then the plaintiff is responsible for the defendant's reasonable attorney's fees and costs IF the case is resolved by a jury verdict at trial.

A plaintiff has thirty days from the date of receipt to accept or reject the defendant's proposal for settlement. If the plaintiff does not accept the offer within thirty days of receipt, it is deemed rejected by law.

This goes both ways. If the plaintiff files a proposal for settlement under the above rules, and a jury verdict **exceeds the plaintiff's offer to settle by 25 percent or more, then the defendant is responsible for all of the plaintiff's attorneys' fees and costs.**

Any proposal for settlement must be in writing and contain the following information:

a) the name of the party to whom the proposal is relevant, along with the party making the proposal,

b) identifying the claims that the proposal concerns,

c) relevant conditions that must be clearly stated for the settlement,

d) the total amount of the settlement along with any non-monetary terms,

e) amount for punitive damages, if any,

f) whether attorneys' fees are included, and

g) a certificate of service that the proposal was sent to the concerned party.

Florida Rule of Civil Procedure 1.442 can push a party just enough to settle a case without costing both parties unnecessary litigation expenses, based on what the parties speculate a jury might do with the facts of a particular cause of action. Plaintiffs should be aware that it's possible to get a verdict, and then owe money to the other side. It's also possible for a plaintiff to obtain a verdict, and have their attorney get paid by the insurance company OR the defendant themselves at a rate higher than the percentage attorney's fee, which also allows the client to receive all or a significant chunk of the entire money judgment.

Let me give you some examples: Let's say that the defendant "Martin" sent a proposal for settlement to the injured plaintiff "Steve" for $100,000 six months prior to the trial. The jury returns a verdict of $70,000 (Steve wins the case). That is less than 75 percent of the $100,000 proposal for settlement. Steve in this situation may have obtained verdict, but now the <u>Martin's attorney</u> can send a bill to the Steve for all of the hours of time they spent litigating the case after the subject proposal for settlement expired. If the defense attorney spent 100 hours and their normal hourly charge is $300 an hour, the Steve actually owes Martin $30,000 in attorney's fees! But then let's say there are $10,000 of additional costs. Then suddenly that $70,000 becomes a verdict of $30,000 when plaintiff Steve could have settled the case 6 months prior for $100,000. That's what I meant when I stated you can win and still lose.

Now counter to that, using the same numbers for a case where plaintiff Steve files a proposal for settlement for $100,000, and the jury returns a verdict for $140,000. That is 25 percent MORE than Steve's proposal for settlement. Now let's use the exact same hours and hourly rate for Steve's attorney. The contingency fee on $140,000 is $56,000. However, the insurance company and/or defendant Martin owes Steve's attorney $30,000 in hourly attorney's fees. So now plaintiff Steve instead of having to pay his attorney $56,000, pays their lawyer $26,000, and the insurance company and/or defendant pays the difference.

This can be useful when the insurance company is being unreasonable, as a way to make it economically worthwhile for the plaintiff and their attorney to take the case to trial. In all fairness, if the insurance company has made a reasonable offer and the plaintiff refuses to settle, there can be serious consequences to the plaintiff for being unreasonable. It's important to have a conversation with your lawyer before going to trial regarding proposals for settlement to ensure that you are making a smart decision to accept or reject an offer. Additionally, there are mechanisms to protect you from these consequences of a proposal for settlement if the decision is a difficult one. Insurance has been created that can actually protect parties in the event of a negative verdict at trial. For more information about Legal Fee Guard, go to www.LegalFeeGuard.com.

MEDIATION

All Florida personal injury claims are required to go to mediation and/or non-binding arbitration before they are allowed to go to trial. These are referred to as "Alternative Dispute Resolution" events (ADR). I will discuss what a mediation is first. This is the best opportunity to settle a case prior to going to trial. It usually happens after all written discovery has been done and the depositions of the plaintiff and the defendant have been taken.

For example, let's say Tom underwent knee surgery after the accident. Tom has gone through physical therapy post-surgery, it's been five months, and his surgeon, Dr. Petty, says his condition is not going to get any better, or any worse. Dr. Petty can give an opinion as to what Tom's medical care will be in the future.

Tom is then at "maximum medical improvement." We have a pretty good idea of what limitations he is going to experience after knee surgery. Tom's situation is a solid example of a claim that is ripe for mediation.

Here's how it works. The mediator is an attorney, and neutral, meaning they do not have any stake in the outcome of the case. The mediator listens to the attorneys for each side give short opening statements, usually around 10 minutes reach, summarizing their cases. Sometimes the attorneys will forward confidential summaries to the mediator in advance.

After both sides present, they are separated into different rooms, for what's called "caucusing." Since 2020, most mediations are done through Zoom or similar virtual platforms, and caucusing is done by putting the parties with their attorneys in separate "break out rooms." Either way, it gives the parties an opportunity to speak with their attorneys privately throughout the proceeding. The mediator goes back and forth between the rooms, delivering demands and offers, back and forth, in an effort to facilitate a settlement. Sometimes there are only a few moves made, but often the sides could go back and forth over 10 times. There is no limit.

There are three ways a mediation ends: 1) a mutually agreed-upon settlement; 2) an impasse, which means the parties were not able to reach an agreement; or there's what's called an "adjournment."

An adjournment allows the defense attorney or adjuster a few days to talk to some of the supervisors with insurance company to get more "authority," meaning the ability to offer more money to the plaintiff. It can also be used if a plaintiff's attorney or the plaintiff themselves need more time to evaluate the offer. Sometimes a plaintiff will want to "sleep on it" before making a decision. Under those circumstances, it can be helpful not to close the book on the mediation. In a worst case scenario, if the sides aren't able to reach an agreement after a few days or a week, you impasse the mediation, and continue pushing the case towards trial.

Anything that transpires or is spoken in the mediation is confidential. If something is said at the mediation, it cannot be used against you. I do, however, tell my clients that when the mediation presentation is going on, it's in their best interest not to react, not to take the bait and start getting defensive. No testimony is taken at mediation. No matter how upset you might get at something the defense attorney has said, you will have an opportunity to vent in private with your attorney when you are in caucus.

Remember, the defense attorney and insurance adjuster are always evaluating you as a witness for trial. You don't want to give them the impression that you would not be likable, relatable, even-tempered, or anything like that to a jury, because that will increase their desire to go to trial.

Even if you don't settle a case at mediation, it's an accomplishment, because you cannot have your case tried in front of a jury unless you first comply with the court's order of having a mediation. Checking the mediation box is another step forward towards the conclusion of your claim one way or another.

Sometimes a case is just not ripe for a settlement at mediation. Often however, a mediation can set up future negotiations, and a case can be resolved by the parties still without going all the way with a jury trial.

NON-BINDING ARBITRATION

This is another form of alternative dispute resolution (ADR) that can be ordered by a judge or the parties can voluntarily submit to it. These procedures are governed by Florida Rule of Civil Procedure 1.820. Just like a regular arbitration, there is an arbitrator and both sides get to present arguments. Parties can choose to have witnesses testify, but often they do not. If they do testify, it is much shorter than if they were testifying in a trial. It is meant to be informal. Attorneys from both sides will submit any documents they want the arbitrator to consider to the arbitrator before the arbitration, or usually within a couple of days of the meeting. Deadlines for submitting materials should be clearly stated by the selected arbitrator. Within 10 days of the non-binding arbitration hearing, the arbitrator must notify the parties of their decision in writing.

Now keep in mind that this is a "non-binding" arbitration, that a standard arbitration where the arbitrator has the final say on the matter. Any party can reject the arbitrator's decision and request a trial if they do so within 20 days of the arbitrator's filed written decision. If neither party objects to the arbitrator's decision, then the decision becomes binding, and the case is over.

If the arbitrator's decision is rejected and the case goes to trial, the consequences are similar to a "proposal for settlement," that I wrote about earlier. To keep it simple, let's use an example of a non-binding arbitration award of $100,000 for the plaintiff. The award is rejected by the plaintiff. The jury returns a verdict of $70,000. In theory, the plaintiff has won the case. But that is less than 75 percent of the $100,000 non-binding arbitration award. So now the defendant's attorney can send a bill to the plaintiff for all of the hours of time they spent litigating the case after the subject after the rejection of the $100,000 award. Again, it is quite similar to a proposal for settlement.

Now let's go the other way. The defendant rejects the $100,000 non-binding arbitration award. The case goes to trial and the jury returns a verdict for $140,000. That is over 25 percent more than the non-binding arbitration award. Now it is the defendant that owes attorney's fees and costs to the plaintiff.

Obviously it is important for plaintiffs to understand the consequences of these procedures. A personal injury attorney should be able to explain this to their client and guide them to make the best decision for them based on the non-binding arbitrator's decision. However, this is an opportunity for both sides to get a neutral, unbiased opinion from someone who has no knowledge of the case prior to the hearing. These types of procedures can help get a case settled for that reason.

YOU'RE GOING TO TRIAL!
WHAT YOU SHOULD KNOW.

Here is some basic advice I would give any injury victim going to trial.

Look like you actually care! Look interested throughout the case. After all, this is your only opportunity. You won't get another chance, so make sure it looks as if you care. Take notes if you want to during the trial. The jury is watching you the entire time. Most of the jurors are not thrilled to be there. You are the most important piece of evidence, so whether or not it looks like you care really does matter. If you look disinterested, why are they going to be interested?

No phones! Turn it off. Put it away. Do not check your phone while court is in session. The jury is not allowed to have their phones on them, and they have to turn them off while the trial is going on, so don't rub it in by looking at your phone while they are there. Your family and friends need to know that you are not available for phone calls and texts while you are sitting in court.

Your body (the main evidence) must be at trial! You also have to consider that many of the jurors do not want to be there, so it is important to them that you be present for the trial. As I said before, they are watching you the whole time. If your testimony is that you have difficulty sitting for more than two hours a time, keep in mind that trial time could be eight hours a day or more; if you sit there the entire time without getting up, without stretching, without going to the bathroom, a juror might notice that. You don't have to ask permission to stretch or go to the bathroom as long as you're not on the stand. It's important to be at the trial, but you're not chained to the chair.

Body language. Your reactions throughout the trial matter, your body language, your facial expressions. You know the defense is going to put up witnesses and experts that are going to say that you're not hurt or you're not hurt from this particular accident. They might even say that you're being untruthful and a liar. An overly dramatic reaction or some type of outburst is not appropriate, and you are shooting yourself in the foot by reacting that way. If you have friends or family in the courtroom, the same applies to them. No outbursts, nothing overly dramatic.

Don't talk to jurors! All lawyers and parties are strictly prohibited from speaking with jurors. The judge will say this multiple times during the trial. If you see a juror in an elevator, wait for the next one. If you bump into a juror in a bathroom, do not speak with them. They understand. You should avoid any and all possibly appearances of impropriety. You're not being rude. It's the rules. If you violate this rule, you can sabotage your case with a mistrial and have to start the trial all over again. So once again, do not talk to jurors!

Do not say insurance! It will cause a mistrial. Forget the word exists during the time of your trial. The jury is not to know whether there is insurance to cover the damages in your case. The only exception would be if you had an uninsured motorist claim, but it's wisest to avoid the word at all costs.

Trust your lawyer. You've come this far. You're a team. You must let your lawyer do their job. Second guessing every move is self-defeating, as it may distract your lawyer from objecting or addressing a matter with the court. If you have questions, write them down and your attorney can answer during a break.

DAMAGES – WHY YOU ARE MAKING A CLAIM!

Damages is legalese for MONEY. Below is the **actual Florida Jury Instruction** for damages in personal injury claims, followed by an explanation about how damages are proven, and why money is awarded.

501.2 PERSONAL INJURY AND PROPERTY DAMAGES: ELEMENTS

*a.	Injury, pain, disability, disfigurement, loss of capacity for enjoyment of life:*

Any bodily injury sustained by (name) **and any resulting pain and suffering [disability or physical impairment] [disfigurement] [mental anguish] [inconvenience] [or] [loss of capacity for the enjoyment of life] experienced in the past [or to be experienced in the future]. There is no exact standard for measuring such damage. The amount should be fair and just in the light of the evidence.**

b.	*Medical expenses:*

Care and treatment of claimant:

The reasonable [value] [or] [expense] of [hospitalization and] medical [and nursing] care and treatment necessarily or reasonably obtained by (claimant) **in the past [or to be so obtained in the future].**

Care and treatment of minor claimant after reaching majority:

> **The reasonable [value] [or] [expense] of [hospitalization and] medical [and nursing] care and treatment necessarily or reasonably to be obtained by** (minor claimant) **after [he] [she] reaches the age of** (legal age).

c. *Lost earnings, lost time, lost earning capacity:*

When lost earnings or lost working time shown:

> **[Any earnings] [Any working time] lost in the past [and any loss of ability to earn money in the future].**

When earnings or lost working time not shown:

> **Any loss of ability to earn money sustained in the past [and any such loss in the future].**

Non-Economic Damages

When people bring a personal injury claim, it's not just about getting your medical bills paid and recovering lost wages. PIP benefits and health insurance will pay for most of your past medical bills. The reason you are consulting with an attorney is to seek compensation for your injuries. This is the focus of Florida Jury Instruction 501.2 (a).

What is going to convince an insurance company or a jury to pay an injury victim to avoid a lawsuit or settle a case? It's money that you are actually going to receive for the pain and suffering, loss of enjoyment of life, permanent injuries, and inconvenience this accident has caused you. It's the impact on a person's life. This is the greatest loss a person usually suffers within a personal injury claim. It's the permanent difference to their lives from the accident.

In order for an injury plaintiff to qualify for non-economic damages for an automobile negligence case, a jury MUST find that a person suffered a ***permanent impairment/injury.*** This is based on the testimony of the

Plaintiff, their doctors, family members, and anyone else that can talk about the impact on the injured person's life. This is ONLY in automobile negligence cases, but not in slip/trip and fall cases and other negligence personal injury actions. Still, a doctor stating that a person has a permanent injury from an incident carries significant weight with a jury.

You may be thinking to yourself, "How the heck does someone calculate those damages?" Truthfully, they are the hardest to explain to a jury. There is no exact formula for calculating these damages. As the instruction says, *"There is no exact standard for measuring such damage. The amount should be fair and just in the light of the evidence."* Commonly, attorneys will make arguments asking for a certain amount of money per day, per week or per year for having to suffer with the pain and ailments caused by an individual or corporate defendant's negligence.

Economic Damages

These are the most straightforward damages to prove and for a jury to understand. They are exact numbers. They are understandable. Jury Instruction 501.2(b) is the first section concerning economic damages, medical expenses.

This instruction asks the jurors to award what they believe is the reasonable amount of money spent in the past for medical bills, and what it will cost the person in medical bills in the future. Juries can look at past medical bills to come up with opinions concerning future medical care. They can also rely on expert witness doctor testimony from the Plaintiff's treating physicians or the defense medical doctors. They are not to consider whether a person has health insurance in almost all situations.

Section 501.2(c) deals with lost income/wages. To successfully make a lost wages claim, the Plaintiff must have been employed at the time of the accident. The attorney will want to look at your past tax returns to make a calculation of money you lost due to not being able to work in the past, and possibly in the future. As mentioned previously, if you have not paid taxes, or if your tax returns are suspicious, DO NOT MAKE A WAGE CLAIM.

PUNITIVE DAMAGES

This is a phrase that is uttered by nonlawyers nonchalantly without really knowing what it means. Punitive damages are not something that you can just plead in a lawsuit. You have to show certain facts to the judge and then the judge has to grant a motion allowing you to pursue a claim of punitive damages. In automobile injury claims, this can come up when you're dealing with a DUI situation. Just because the judge allows you to bring a count for punitive damages does not mean that you've automatically won. You still have to prove them in front of a jury.

An interesting wrinkle to this is that the jury that hears the punitive damages case most likely is not the jury that will hear the underlying trial. For example, if you are dealing with personal injuries stemming from a car accident caused by a drunk driver, your attorney will not be able to say that you were hit by a drunk driver in the underlying car accident causing an injury trial. The punitive damages count—that might be heard by a different jury—comes after you are successful for the initial reason for the lawsuit.

JURY DUTY IS PATRIOTIC

Whenever I have a panel brought into a courtroom I ask them, "Who was excited about receiving their summons to report to jury duty?" Most of the time, nobody raises their hands.

Let's face it. Jury duty is inconvenient. It's not something that anybody really wants to do. But it is necessary to uphold the democracy of the United States of America. The "Bill of Rights" of the U.S. Constitution guarantees the right to a jury of your peers for Americans in civil lawsuits.

If you're not serving in the military, there's really no other way that you can truly serve your country and protect democracy other than serving on a jury. I know all the jokes about getting off of jury duty, but think about this the next time you get a jury summons, and remember that the power really is with the people.

JURY SELECTION

Jury selection makes or breaks a case. It's a fascinating psycho-logical exercise.

A panel of six jurors in Florida decide a personal injury dispute. The Court brings twenty to thirty people into the courtroom for a standard personal injury case like a car accident. The attorneys begin the **Voir Dire**, the jury selection process. But really, it's a "jury de-selection" process.

Attorneys try to determine through their multiple questions (that could take hours, if not days, to complete) whether a potential juror is biased. The attorneys want to know if potential jurors brought in by the Court can be fair and impartial concerning the specific set of facts. A juror might be able to sit and be fair and impartial for one type of case, but possibly not on another. That's what the jury selection process is all about.

If bias is determined by one of the attorneys, there are two different ways to remove someone from a jury panel. The first way is "striking for cause." If somebody flat-out says that they can't be fair and impartial to one of the parties, well, then that prospective juror should not be sitting on the panel at the end of the day.

The other way is "peremptory challenges." In Florida, each side gets three peremptory challenges, meaning that the attorney can strike a person for any reason, as long as it is not race-related. If, for example, a potential juror is wearing a scowl on their face only when one attorney is talking, but they haven't said anything that would strike them off the panel, that attorney might want to strike this person from the panel using a peremptory challenge. Again, each side only gets three, and most attorneys feel like they never have enough.

Pay close attention during this process. You can and should help your attorney by observing the panel, watching their body language and demeanor, and taking notes. This is how you show involvement with your case even before a jury has been chosen. The Defendant and their attorney will be watching you, as well.

What I generally tell a prospective juror panel is that we are trying to find out if one of the parties is might start out a little bit behind the other when the case begins. It's like running a race, and the evidence is the race. Fairness says both parties must start at the same starting line.

JURY VERDICT

After both sides have given a closing argument, the judge reads the final jury instructions the attorneys have agreed on, which the jury gets a printed copy of along with the verdict form.

The jury leaves their phones, personal belongings, and other items on their chairs and goes into the secluded deliberation room. The jury elects a leader, known as the foreperson, and they figure out what they can unanimously agree upon should be the result of your case. This could take ten minutes, it could take days, but it must be unanimous.

In Florida, once they all agree on a decision, it's written down by the foreperson on the verdict form, the jury returns to the courtroom, and the judge's clerk reads the form aloud. The judge will then poll the jury, asking each of them individually, "Is this your verdict?" Then the jury is excused.

The jury, not the judge, has the final say in civil cases, and this is sacred in our country. Our justice system may not be perfect, but few countries allow other citizens to arbitrate disputes like we do in the United States. The President of the United States could walk into a courtroom and say, "I want the defendant to win." It doesn't matter. Whatever the jury decides, there is nothing any judge or any other leader can do to pierce the sanctity of the jury's decision. This right is mandated by the 7th Amendment to the United States Constitution.

Both sides do have an opportunity to appeal jury verdicts, but most of the time, the jury's verdict is upheld by appellate courts.

　　　Jeff Adelman, B.C.S., Esq.

AFTERWORD

I hope you have found this guide helpful, giving you an idea of what you should expect from a personal injury lawyer in the event you need to hire one. The information in this book has been invaluable for me in my practice in general, but of course, every case is different, and reading this book does not make you a lawyer. Read the book, and make a decision as to who is going to handle your case, and follow their advice. I cannot emphasize enough that if you have any doubts about whether you have a claim, you should call a lawyer. It costs you nothing to learn about your rights as all personal injury lawyers offer a free consultation to discuss your matter, and what may appear to be a minor injury initially sometimes turns into something far more serious.

I encourage you to check out my podcast, "Personal Injury Claims with Jeff Adelman," on your favorite podcasting service, where I continue to educate the public about various claim-related injury subjects, as well as offer insurance tips. Put your smartphone camera on the QR code here to access it through Apple Podcasts:

Have more questions? Feel free to drop me a line at Jeff@LawBNI.com For more information about my firm, go to www.LAWBNI.COM.

Jeffrey "Jeff" Adelman is a Martindale Hubbell AV Rated, Florida Bar Board Certified Trial Lawyer who fights for injury victims throughout the Sunshine State and Illinois. He is a member of the Florida Bar, Illinois Bar, the United States Supreme Court Bar, and the Federal Bar for the Southern District and Middle District of Florida.

He was voted "Best Attorney in Coral Springs/Parkland" by the readers of the Coral Springs/Parkland Forum for 12 consecutive years.

He is the past-chair of the Florida Bar Client's Security Fund and Past-President of the Fort Lauderdale Chapter of the American Board of Trial Advocates (ABOTA) for 2020. Jeff served as President of statewide ABOTA (FLABOTA) for 2023-24.

Jeff, originally from Chicago, has been a part of the City of Coral Springs (Florida) community since 1985. He is a partner with Brotman Nusbaum Ibrahim & Adelman and the main office for the firm is out of Boca Raton. When he isn't fighting for injured peoples' rights, he enjoys spending time with his wife Jessica and their sons, Benjamin and Jacob, reading, community involvement, and cheering on the Chicago Blackhawks and Florida Panthers.

Made in the USA
Columbia, SC
05 May 2025